The Sound of Heart Is Here I Am

The Sound of Heart Is Here I Am

Poems by

Ann Iverson

© 2026 Ann Iverson. All rights reserved.
This material may not be reproduced in any form, published,
reprinted, recorded, performed, broadcast,
rewritten or redistributed without
the explicit permission of Ann Iverson.
All such actions are strictly prohibited by law.

Cover design by Shay Culligan
Cover image by Birger Strahl

ISBN: 978-1-63980-854-0
Library of Congress Control Number: 2026931988

Kelsay Books
502 South 1040 East, A-119
American Fork, Utah 84003
Kelsaybooks.com

for Jack, Arline, Jeannie, Claudia, Margie, and Mary

Acknowledgments

Thank you to the following publications, in which versions of these poems previously appeared:

Amaranth Journal: "Once Upon a Time: Red Owl Grocery Store"

Anti Heroin Chic: "What I Liked Most"

Kosmeo!: "Y," "Happiness"

The Penwood Review: "Namesake," "Heaven"

Poetry Box: Off-Topic Publishing: "Certainly"

Prachya Review: "Royal"

Spirit Fire Review: "Dear Elle,"

Urban Planning Poetry Zine: "Y," "Royal"

Special thanks to Deborah Keenan for manuscript arrangement and general edits.

The guardians to this book are Rita Moe, Marie Rickmyer, Teresa Boyer, Liz Wier, and Tracy Youngbloom, and all the members of Deborah Keenan's Monday poetry class.

Contents

DOWN A RIVER NAMED DELIGHT

Road Trip	15
What I Liked Most	16
It Really Doesn't Matter	20
When Sorrow Sits with Me	22
I Am Four	23
Love's Manifesto	24
Driving North, Thanksgiving Day	26
Take Me as I Am	27
By Mistake, I	28
The Fidelity of Squirrels	30
206 Westchester Drive	32
I Pledge Allegiance	34

DUSTY MOONLIGHT AND A GOLDEN GHOST

Road Trip	37
Namesake	38
Heaven	39
Heaven, Again	41
Tonight	42
The Order of Things	43
Winter's Window	44
The Poem Is Open for Business	46
Ars Poetica	47
Shadows	48
Falling	50

TO FLY OVER THE HOUSES OF MY HEART

Road Trip	53
Snowless Solstice and the Red Bird Visits	54
Blue Collar	55
Once Upon a Time: Red Owl Grocery Store	56
Partial Portrait of My Parents and One Closet	57
Dear Sister,	58
October	59
Dear Elle,	60
Lesson	61
Right now,	62
Alive on Earth	63
The Hilarity of Death	64
Dear Macy's,	65
Birthday Visitation	67
Family Affair	68
Tenderness	70

A LAKE AS CLEAR AS YESTERDAY

Road Trip	73
The Family of God	74
Y	76
Certainly	78
Trees	79
Filling Out a Form Called Homesick	80
November Night	81
41005 Fahrion Road	82
The New Neighbors	84

The Royal 85
May 86
Heart Math 87

EVERY PAINTING HAS A DOOR

Road Trip 91
Yellow 92
Museum Study 93
Blood Work 94
A Man We Used to Know 95
Un 97
Narrative 98
Another Take at Happiness 99
Happiness 101
Notes for Survival 103
Memory 104
Song of July 105
I Am Tired of Perfection 106

Notes 109

DOWN A RIVER NAMED DELIGHT

Road Trip

I'd like to take a road trip down a river named *Delight,* under clouds picked one by one, beneath a sky that knows the past, past the house I rented years ago with a crumbled path and a wall that held the story of how my family moved me in and three weeks later out because I thought the house was haunted and they believed me. I might rent a room with a deer head in the lobby and name the deer, *The Other Side of Things.* In the morning, I wake to sunlight on my pillow and a cat sprawled in the window with one paw on the bright side of my life. Then on the barren road, I'll find a tiger walking back and forth towards the future down a lane named *How Could I Forget?* I could visit the consignment store where my mother sold antiques and near the dusty storefront, I might run into her ghost. I might ask her all the questions I never thought to ask then tell her how nice it was to see her face at last.

What I Liked Most

about the old life
is that it was before
this happened and
after that happened
and in between
all the happenings
that seem to happen.
Like the time the dogs
dragged in a dead
rabbit and how
I screamed and threw
a blanket over it
and hauled it to the back.

Or how people paraded
past with kids or dogs
or babies in strollers
or how, if I fell
asleep on the old blue couch,
I could see the moon floating
through the pines and hear the
owl's distant hoot.

What I liked most
about the old life
is that she wasn't sick
and he could still walk
and you and you and you
were still alive.
And still, we haven't
finished saying
our goodbyes.

What I liked most
about the old life
is that the phone
was attached to the wall.
The TV had five channels
and I licked a stamp
to pay the bills
and sewed pillows
on the porch.

What I liked most
about the old life
is that I can't seem
to grab it. It's like
one of those games
at the State Fair
when you try to clutch
a prize with a mechanical
wench but you only get
what you can get.

What I liked most
about the old life
is that it wasn't old at all
but big as a dream,
enormous as a wish
when you throw
pennies in a fountain.
You see its reflection
across the pools
of water and wonder
where it went.

What I liked most
about the old life
is when I painted
all the garden statues
gold, and they shimmered
in the sun and the cat
sat in the window
and the neighbors
waved and pointed
and I felt as though
I was good.

It Really Doesn't Matter

A man was so in love with you
that when you parted, he moved
to the woods and carved
your name into pieces of bark
then sent a letter to tell you so,
That really doesn't matter now.
Nor do the glass lanterns
that need batteries all the time
nor the unreconciled rooms of the heart.
It really doesn't matter if you make
cheesy potatoes the day before
or the morning of, they taste the same
either way. And what about those old
memories of betrayal? They can sit
cold stone in the basement;
just close the fruit cellar door.
The rainy road says *but everything matters.*
Who can argue with a rainy road?
Those dreams when love comes back to you;
you'd think they'd matter but they don't.
One day the trees went on forever
about what matters and what does not?

Then the darkest day of the year
said *I really try to matter
but for some, I know I don't.*
If you eat on dirty dishes
that really doesn't matter because
some eat off the floor. Or some eat
not at all. The stories hiding inside you
sometimes matter too much.
When silence eats away, the industrious
sound of the pileated matters just a little.
But the story of the barred owl who flew
in through a chimney, then perched atop
the glittering tree.
That one matters most.

When Sorrow Sits with Me

The heavy sky
and darkened days

call out to us
as we sit beneath a tree.

She takes my hand;
I pull away

yet follow her down a path
of broken limbs and tarnished leaves

and all water from the streams.
She points to a train that contains my loves;

as it pulls away
she whispers *I am here to stay.*

I Am Four

sitting plump
on the summer sidewalk
in a yellow frilly dress
picking up a June bug
mistaken for a sweet.
Grandpa comes home
from Mexico
with a knapsack packed
with fancy pinwheel toys
and photos of himself
beside a swordfish
twice as tall as he.
The next year on my birthday
he passed
to the other side.
We had balloons, cake,
a teddy bear
named Guss.
Mother wore
a green and pink
polka-dotted dress
sat on a chair
buried her face
in a white apron
made of lace.

Love's Manifesto

i

All because calamity
didn't escape from
grief's hold, I
just knew love
might never open
like a page or a question
like a reckless saturated
tomorrow, an unclaimed
vacancy. What?
Then someone
finished my sentence.
XYZ.

ii

Zinnias say *yes*
to the X in XO. Why
would I voluntarily unleash
your tremble today? Love's symmetry
remembers the quackery of
the permanent *Oh* of no man's land.
Its knowledge justifies inhibition.
Have I gone mad forever?
Enough of the demand.
Love starts like this:
caution, burn, adore.

Driving North, Thanksgiving Day

Along the way, Hopper houses
dot the land with white
in barren fields of gray.
Silos isolated
in their own opinions
stand up for what they believe.
Gravestones align in perfect rows
as though grief
has anything to do with order.
Corner cafes gather dust
in lonely, languid towns.
Headlights of a train
brighten the wayward forward.
Every horizon in the mirror
is much farther than it appears.

Take Me as I Am

Self Portrait with Pipe and Straw Hat
Oil on Canvas, Vincent Van Gogh

If it were not for my tangled times of torment.
If it were not for the great fire in my heart.
See how my eyes glow like rolling meadows?
If it were not for this mind that thinks in living color.
I wish you could only take me as I am.
I am a ghost now, am I not?
Yet, I am everywhere.
I float within the space
of what is tangled, what unravels
a glowing everywhere.

By Mistake, I

spread the wildflower seeds
not according to instructions.
Though that's not really true.
I read the bag but thought
wild and *according to*
just will never do.
So, with half the bag,
I followed the rules:
raked the dirt
and scattered.
The other half
I didn't.

I threw the rest
into the air
and shouted
congratulations,
my very best wishes,
hats off to you
I hope you
make it through.

The Fidelity of Squirrels

In the city, deer roamed the rim of shadows.
Turkeys clamored their worth.
A great horned stood guard on the lamppost,
and a coyote circled my car at the park.
The hawk nested in the tree.
A raccoon wobbled up the walk
as though he came to call.
A goose flew by for daily feedings
as did mallards, as did ducks.
A fox darted down the path
while finches and jays
threw their song to the air.

But out here way north of the lights,
deep in the darkness of the woods,
all I see are squirrels.
Squirrels. Squirrels. Squirrels—
        chasing through the trees,
swinging from branch to branch
           eating up the corn.
I thank them for their comical crusade,
their movement, their headway,
their progress to survive, for shattering apathy's glass.

Desperate for soft brown eyes, I bought buck and doe decoys.
Put them together and hauled them through the trees.
Someone took a picture of me and sent it to a friend
who said I looked like a James Bond girl in the woods
in my black boots, coat, pants. From my winter window,
I can see them and even though they cannot move,
I imagine that they can.

206 Westchester Drive

I grew up two doors down from a taxidermist who threatened to stuff our cat and kittens if they ever entered his yard. He'd shake his rifle and stomp to his lawn chair to patrol his .15acre lot. The house between ours and his was a house of fair-haired girls with flawless skin, fluttery eyes, fine hearts, and a mother who failed at forty-five. On the other side, lived a mysterious family whose mother starved her girl, who was taken away and never brought back on a bleak November day. In the month of May, her husband drove his blue GTO out of town and put a bullet through his head. The next house had three boys: two of them were artists. We'd drink Kool-Aid and draw for hours on their picnic table in the shade and in the sun. When their parents divorced, the woman painted her nails and dyed her hair bright red. Across the street and kitty-corner lived a family who seemed to have it all. At Christmas, they displayed their unwrapped gifts under the tree for days and days on end. To their right lived the taxidermist's brother. They feuded for years; sometimes we heard their banters echo down the street. The brother who did not stuff dead animals hanged himself in his garage.

In my house lived five daughters, a milkman, and his wife. Our yard in June was yellow with weeds, embarrassed I'd cut their tops off with a clipper. Rodgers and Hammerstein filled the air, while my dad read books, and my mom polished old furniture from the antique store. Our love was beautiful, betrayed, bountiful, bruised, beyond believable, an unbelievably bated biography, with secrets, not told here, but as messy as the rest.

I Pledge Allegiance

to the sky and all the stars inside
to jets that rumble
through its veins
to birds and blues and Goodyear blimps
to helicopters that chop the air in half
to flocks of geese that fill the void
while they honk and say goodbye.

I pledge allegiance to the ground
to dirt and mud and rolling hills
to fields of sugarcane
to earthworms tunneling
through tangled roots
and jumbled worth
it's mucky girth
to catch us
when and where we fall.

DUSTY MOONLIGHT AND A GOLDEN GHOST

Road Trip

Yes, I'd like to take a road trip to circle back around to the door that I let love in while the barge sings out its song. I might pull over for a picnic with an owl who *hoos* a message to the moon and a hare with droopy ears named S*orrow One* and *Sorrow Two*. I might take a road trip to the city named *Be Careful* and spend the night swimming in a pool filled with only air. In the morning when I wake, I'll be floating on tomorrow. I could drive some more along the river's edge and run into a love who took his life so long ago. I won't ask him why; his reasons will not matter but his eyes will fill with water, floating pieces of the sun. I'll spend the night curled up in a ditch of dusty moonlight while a golden ghost floats over spreading starlight in my hair.

Namesake

God, how shall I call to you
when you float through the rafters
like a ghost with no name?

I must rename you
but can't seem to find the right word
am too tired to make one up.

It must be as heavy as iron
yet light as a broken wing
on the walk.

The word must be damaged
to make any sense
must be whole to endure the change.

Heaven

God buys a new robe,
black velvet piped in gold,

deep pockets to keep his lists
of all the things he needs to do.

Mary sews a maternity cloak
readying for the second coming

of Christ whose hands and feet
have finally healed from

the first time he came
to save us from our sins.

The streets are cobbled
in one long and winding road.

A different song takes over the air.
Cats brush legs

of patron saints
push quills and ink

off of Joseph's
new desk

where he draws a map
for the Savior

so he knows how
to find us again.

Heaven, Again

The doors are not of gilded gold
but bluebirds floating in a boat.
Lamps are shaped like owls;
with shades of woven stories.

The ceiling fans have chains
with diamond-studded charms.
When you pull them
poems not air fly out.

The walls are lined with a musical score
composed by Starlight Sleeping.
On his lap, Christ holds
a redwood box

safekeeping the letters
you could not bear to write.
Like paper dolls, the dead line up
and God gives you clothes to dress them.

Tonight

I want to buy the moon
a super one for me
a harvest one for you.

Tomorrow, I want
to eat the sun
drenched
in a bowl full
of yes.

The Order of Things

Are you a goose finding its place
in the metaphoric arrow?

Or the grey wolf
of a Libra's heart?

Do you rotate your head almost full circle?
If so, what will your vision be?

Do you turn left like a bat when you leave your home?
How far will you fly from your life?

Is your heart in your head like a squid's?
That might not be a bad thing.

If you can sleep for three years like a snail,
then tell me all your dreams.

Winter's Window

Winter's Window
Painting by Jef Bourgeau

I

It's large with one sheer curtain
pushed to the side.
It appears that it might be open
so light and dark can pour in.
The Moon
floats by like a barge.
Trees light up in fire with flames
not red but white.
We know there's a path through the snow,
so, someone either came or left.
If you look hard enough
you might find that person's ghost.

II

My winter window
is a painting too.
One red shed, one black road,
one beige house, with an arched window
an occasional interesting bird
that I refuse to name.
If you look hard enough
you'll find that nothing
stays the same.

The Poem Is Open for Business

They borrowed funds from the Mercantile Bank and set up shop on the corner of Iamb and Enjambment. They are open yesterday, today, and tomorrow and sell words on strings like pearls but at three times the regular price. The owner is an art historian but formally a cardiac nurse. She knows the sound of a heart in distress and will count beats at the counter while she wraps your stanzas in parchment paper and wired velvet ribbon. They do not accept returns even if you have a receipt but will issue a credit voucher if the language is dented or cracked. On Wednesdays, they offer slant rhymes for 59 cents a piece. On Fridays, they open their backroom for revisions, spread out butcher paper, and hand you a carving knife.

Ars Poetica

Give me a poem
that tells a true story
like how the moon
found her light.

I need a poem like
a boat without an anchor
where the waters stir the oar.

Poems
should be cut and bruised
bitten and beaten,
learn resuscitation
and how to drive
in the dark.

Give me a poem that purrs
like the motor
of a baby's dream
or one that tells a lie
then darts off
like a rabbit so,
you can never
find it again.

Shadows

They meet at midnight to tell their stories
of what it's like to always follow.

What they followed and how they followed
and how they wanted more.

When darkness speaks
they take dictation

and stroll museums after hours
to study their worth and installation.

On the moon, they gather
in their smokey suits.

If you look up,
you can see them.

They translate light and lay beside you
invisible while you dream.

When weary of their ashen skin
they paint themselves bright red.

They are more perfect
than what precedes them.

Falling

for G

I am the tree
home to a trillion wings
moss on my back
owls in my hollowed spaces.
A swing on my arm
the weight of a human
who plants flowers
at my feet.
I am you with a thousand limbs.
From me, everything must fall.
Like the young man
whose neck snapped on the ground.
I watched him drop and
had God granted me permission
to move my arms
I would have scooped him up
to save him.

TO FLY OVER THE HOUSES
OF MY HEART

Road Trip

Or I might end up in my mother's kitchen while she holds the plate before me, and my father strokes my hair. I could decide to walk along the burrows of my past and find a lion whose eyes are dark, his tail, a ladder to the sun. I might climb it rung by rung and find a brush to paint my way and name the burning portrait *I'll Love You 'til the End.* If I tire of walking, I might decide to fly over the houses of my heart where all the roofs are gardens and the sky is lined in gold. I could take a needle and mend the past or sew the clouds together as a quilt to keep me warm. I might get too bold and fly too high, leaving what I know and find myself becoming a ring around Neptune. If my wings become too weak, I might decide to swim and meet a whale with pale blue eyes and learn the language of the deep.

Snowless Solstice and the Red Bird Visits

When I close my eyes
and open them, I see
my father, my cat, my baby, my mother:
gifts from the ruby herald.
When I dream, my father is
dying his second death.
My dead cat alive in the reverie
is curled around his head.
When I drive my car
my baby comes to me.

Since she left
before she could ever learn to read,
she reads me into privacies
that no one else could ever.
With her small hands,
she scans my face
as though it were a book of braille.
My mother dressed
as a beautiful ghost
turns every single page.

Blue Collar

Father was a boat of promises
        some he kept
          along the river's edge

where he delivered milk
        to those who had much less
        than we had ever had.

His veins were cerulean, cramps cobalt
        indigo eyes,
        a sapphire heart.

In his uniform of royal trousers and a periwinkle shirt
        he trudged
        through mud, sleet, dirt.

At home at the kitchen table
        he smoked, sighed, drank coffee
        boiled with grinds and egg.

I do not know what he dreamed of;
        I would be a sinner
        to make it up.

I like to think he rode a horse
        a wild one
        painted by Marc.

Once Upon a Time: Red Owl Grocery Store

Every Friday when my dad got paid,
he'd hand the check over to my mom
and she'd walk to the bank to deposit it
then walk to Red Owl for groceries.
All of us would follow.
In the old brown sedan, my dad
would pick us up.
One package of maple-flavored cookies
was all that was allowed.
I liked how they were shaped like a leaf
and would lick the frosting from around the edge.
They'd be gone in an hour.
Then that was that. Potato chips were reserved
for Christmas with French onion dip.
Saltines were plenty, we'd eat them
with butter and parmesan cheese.
The owl had a friendly happy face
one that I could trust. One that I adored.

Partial Portrait of My Parents and One Closet

Their fighting was rare but when they did
we'd hide in the closet, a place
of mysterious objects:
red rubber hot water bottle, outdated
encyclopedia, umbrella, golf clubs,
bowling ball, work boots, box
of purple plastic window beads,
badminton set, winter coat
with fur trim. Sometimes
when waiting for the silence,
I'd organize the shoes.

Dear Sister,

The moon has vanished into January, but the road where I find you will never disappear. Rivers rage—fires roar. A Black Hawk collides with a plane carrying a host of tiny ones who dance on ice, then pour into the Potomac. People have no homes. I wish I had a cat. Your son changed his Facebook photo to you and him when you were well. TIKTOK has drowned like a big bear in someone's evacuated pool. I know it might not interest you but I don't even like to vote. Everyone hates each other. It's this side or that. I have a war story I never told you and can't even tell you here. I hope it's warm in Heaven. If not, I will send a shawl. I hope your wings are made of pearls and diamond-studded lace. When you talk to God, please tell him what to do.

October

I can barely
watch the leaves
leap from the branch
as though to take
their little leafy lives.

Can barely light
enough candles at night
or drag the sweaters out.

Can barely stop thinking
of a friend
whose memory escapes
one tale at a time.

Whose desperate
phone calls are filled
with the same
childhood stories
re-told and re-told.

I can barely
stand to listen.
I can barely
stand to not.

Dear Elle,

I'm not sure why you changed your name from Karen or why you wore pearls even to the beach. I'm not sure why you had so much hair or how it cascaded when you finally fell and perished alone in your condo, adorned all in off-white. Those lovely blond locks must have haloed your head as, daily you lay on the floor with no one in sight. Did you mean it when you asked me to visit with my two dogs? Did you know they would only wreak havoc on your ivory white tower? This is not to say that your seclusion was privileged; it's only to say you wore black dresses with Italian-made boots and took long naps on a cream-colored sofa, piled high with cream-colored throws and shams. One time you made me a lunch and served it on fine china at a park across from my work. You rode an electric bike downtown wearing sexy sundresses, platform sandals, and designer sunglasses. Your fireplace mantel at Christmas was better than the White House. I'll never understand when you came back from that culinary class in Rome and invited me over for fancy cuisine, then served me White Castle straight from the fridge. Some things go right over my head. When you called me late at night or early in the morning, I hope you know I was only half awake. As I listened to your pleas for me to come with my stinky dogs, I knew it would not be a good plan. So instead, I sent you an oversized teddy bear, making sure that its fur was cream, paws were cream, its bow was cream, as cream as the dream I had the night you died, as you floated over my bed.

Lesson

Today my sister sent a video
of a piliated woodpecker
pecking the shape
of a heart into an oak
along the river's edge.
With such intention
he carved the form—
nothing random to it.

A funny feathery artist
with great vision for the tree
who stood proud with patience
as the bird chiseled his dream.
What mystery there is
in such purpose and aim.

Right now,

I am writing a blog about selecting industrial window blinds for a modern space. From the garage, I hear my husband practicing the eulogy for his brother whose brain was sacrificed suddenly to stroke. He has revised his message at least 500 times and is now reciting it out loud to his dog who I imagine is tilting his head in question. He's at the part where he tells how they hunted pheasants with stones and sticks when Brooklyn Center was farmland. He moves on to their annual deer hunting trips. *You can be sure there will be an empty chair for him at the campfire this year.* He ends, *I've always said that if dogs aren't in Heaven, I'm not going. I can see my brother smiling now sitting up there with Gunner and Jet.* Sometimes I think the heart has to be as tall as Abraham Lincoln, as smart as Benjamin Franklin, as brave as Amelia Earhart, as beautifully bold as Frida Kahlo.

Alive on Earth

After his send-off, we take the long way home:
fields swaying tall with corn, a rusty swing set
abandoned on the hill, winding roads a mirage
of what's to come, tips of sumac wet with red
like slender quills dipped in ink
writing love letters to the dead.

Two bucks run along a line of pines,
then disappear over the knoll into the grove.
I say, *That's your dad and brother.*
I ask, Even if it's not, what's left
if you can't believe in signs like that?

Being deserted alive on earth is a funny way to be.
We'll do anything to make the dead stay
closer. For me when I need to choose a color—
it's purple for mom and green for dad.

The living will believe in anything. That bird
must be your sister. Your friend, the flickering
light. Your husband climbs the rainbow and is
quickly out of sight. You miss a call at 3:00 am;
you know it was your wife.

The Hilarity of Death

When my mother passed,
I went on a shopping spree:
One sweater dress (canary yellow),
hot pink tights (I thought would match),
a pair of wedged vintage sandals, a used
crock pot (in good condition), three
new purses, powder blue eye shadow,
Cover Girl blush, bright red lipstick, an
antique quilt, Sally Hanson nail fortifier,
eyebrow pencil sharpener, leopard print
floor mats, and a new litter box.
I packed my car with shit
to make me feel alive.

Dear Macy's,

In my inbox today, I received a message from you that read: *Want to pause Mother's Day emails? We understand that this time of year can be difficult for some. If you'd like to take a break from getting our Mother's Day emails this year, just click here.* I started to think about all the other holidays that aren't a good time of year. Like the Fourth of July for the woman whose mother was struck by a car a week before fireworks exploded in the sky with grief so brilliant that even the crowds could not keep up. Or for the young girl whose mum fell down a flight of stairs in her new high heels and red Christmas dress, coming to greet the party. Grief too, was immaculately conceived—its mother a dark ghost alone and in hiding. Or the man's mamma who jumped from a bridge a day after Palm Sunday. Only grief is as holy as Christ. You can crucify it and be rest assured that on the third day, it will float out of its tomb and find you again.

Oh, Macy's, you got this wrong. I still like you, though, and I used to stroll your aisles looking for clearance earrings and purses. My mother liked you too but only when your name was Dayton's. Every Monday night, she'd steal away on the old Blue Gitney to downtown St. Paul, where she would meet you like a lover, scoping out your racks and keeping an eye on a forty-dollar sweater until it was marked down to four. They were always purple, not red like her sister wore. Oh, Macy's, because of you, my mother had a secret, second life. She died two days before MLK Day, and we buried her in a cashmere coat the same color as a plum.

Birthday Visitation

In the dream, my mother was a sculptor
who carved an ancient city
with winding stairs, temples, turrets, grief
beyond control.

She showed me her chisel and mallet
her diamond-studded blade.
She wore a white coat
and a French man's beret.

I woke to
pterodactyl
garbage trucks
shrieking through
the air.

Family Affair

Dad watched *Mister Ed*
and sang
a horse is a horse's ass of course.

One sister flipped
her hair
like Marlo Thomas.

Another wore
a slinky
Ginger dress.

Third sister had freckles
and a darling
Opie face.

Sister number four
had eyes
as big as Bambie's

I wore pigtails like Buffy
with a gap
between my teeth.

Mother was Bewitched
who floated

everything we needed
directly to her side.

When she called out
it's vacuum time
we turned the tube up louder
pretending not to hear.

Tenderness

was born
in a field
when
the mother
died
the father
carried
the small
thing
home.

A LAKE AS CLEAR AS YESTERDAY

Road Trip

The next town that I visit might have no name at all but a lake as clear as yesterday, and I'll spend hours in the sand writing letters never written and watch as they dissolve while the waves pull in and out. I could always drive through mountain valleys and meet angels on their way to pull someone from disaster, then rent a truck and pick up loads of memory, find my father's ghost shoveling up his share. His hair is sandy grey and eyes as soft as fur. He might not be aware of who I really am, so I will just remember *the sound of heart is here I am*. I might stop at the market where they sell hours by the pound then make some bread that calls for time then slowly bake the years and bring it to a friend.

The Family of God

His cousin was a part-time magician
who he consulted when he created the world.

When he watched the rabbit jump out of the hat,
he said, *That's nice. Let's do another trick.* So,

they levitated a woman and taught monarchs how to fly.
They looked at a heart and gave it four rooms,

a perfect house that beats. They trained geese
to form an arrow, hummingbirds to hover,

bats to hang upside down. When he broke his arm
Adam reached out.

His brother was a lawyer. When God was in trouble,
he bailed him out. His mother wore purple. His father was dead.

His sister was a poet and named all the angels one by one,
rearranged the stars and turned them into rhymes.

When he was a boy, he fished on a river, named it
tomorrow, then changed his mind and named it *today.*

Y

In my forest, I have a tree
whose trunk splits near the sky
to form a perfect sans-serif Y.
And though I prefer serifs
on all my letters from A to Z
I'll take what I can see today
my own anointed Y.

On this paper, it's a tiny mantel
where on top I place a candle,
some books between two ends,
a statue of an angel,
and a photo of a friend.

In my forest,
the other trees
turn to it for answers.
Y must we lose our leaves?
Y do we have to grow so old?
Y are we used for fire?

From my window for this page,
I study Y's anatomy.
It's outstretched arms and sturdy stem
of it, I ask it nothing
but give praise for *yes* and *yet.*

Certainly

Such a nice word, so pleasing, so pleasant, so much better than yes.

Can I have the last half of your donut? Certainly! Will you start your hair on fire? Certainly, shouts the tree in October sun.

Less complicated than undoubtedly and even more certain than sure. Unquestionably superior to absolutely. I am most certain of this. It spreads goodness over the land; in spring, each bud is witness to that.

Will some things shatter the heart forever? Unmistakably, undeniably, certainly so. Unequivocally call the dead from the skies. Up here, hearts are not made from glass. Certainly, certainly, certainly so.

Trees

I like trees best naked
when their clothes
have fallen to the ground
as they stand unashamed
in winter sun.

I like that they
don't expect
repayment
when we cut
them down
and bejewel them
with glitter, bulb,
and glow.

I like dark trees
of the forest
that look like
women hiding.

Filling Out a Form Called Homesick

Filing for homestead at the beginning of the year
and I glance out the window at the angels in the garden
and whisper to myself *where's my second life?*
Do you occupy this home? Somewhat, sort of, only with
a half of heart. One leg in and one leg out.
I scatter corn to feed the birds hoping a deer
might find its way. *Did you homestead your previous home?*
I don't remember, but there's no box for that.
The lawn chairs are piled with snow
and one angel has no wings. A metal flamingo
leans against an oak. The antique birdcage is empty,
wire feeders just the same.
Do you certify that the above information
is true and correct?
I have lied in poems before, but not this time.
A stack of dead branches waits to be aflame—
their second life, not mine.

November Night

Hear the hallowed silence
—do not
step into the dark
—leaves will
break from trees.
Memories
will fall.

Watch the moon
balance on
a branch.
The tree has
no idea
how strong
it is
to hold
up all
the light.

41005 Fahrion Road

It's January 29th, 55 degrees.
The grass on the hill is green.
Amazon delivered
a bunch of things I don't need,
and I'll probably order more.
An imposter ladybug
climbs the pane, falls to the sill,
and lands on her back.
I do nothing to assist.
A squirrel scurries up
the fake buck's leg
then jumps to the doe's hind end.
One small wind could push it
all to the ground.

Now the imposter is back on all fours
or sixes I should say.
I wonder how she managed that.
I wonder if she has a heart.
I wonder what it's like to pretend
you're something you're not.
The clouds glide over the sun
or is it the sun floats behind the clouds?
Either way, suddenly
everything is sad.

The New Neighbors

The next-door neighbor kids come on bikes to find me in the garden to say hello and ask if I would buy flowers for a fastpitch fundraiser. Yes, and ask their names: I'm Logan. I'm Alissa. I used to be an English teacher and Alissa says, with her hand on her hip, Oh I didn't know that which made me smile since how would she? Logan grins and says I bet your class was fun; mine is boring and I always fall asleep. I think to myself I was a good teacher and my class was fun. I taught blue-collar men in tool belts and soiled Carhartts how to read a book. I helped them understand Chief and McMurphy and watched their faces freeze when I explained as best I could about lobotomies and Electric Shock Therapy. When I taught them poems, I'd laugh out loud as they cocked their heads, leaned back, and threw their legs up on a chair. It wasn't long until they'd raise their hands to read—their calloused, rustic voices reciting verse as soft as air. Do you want to see what I've been working on in the garden? Of course, we've been watching you. This house used to be beautiful years ago, but then a hoarder moved in. The man behind you will cut down trees for free. He's really nice; you just have to ask. That's good to know; I'm not used to it out here. I hear the interstate all the time. Oh, that's all right; after a while all you'll hear are birds.

The Royal

At the back of this acreage
is a twelve-foot bear carved from oak
fallen over backward
in the mud and leaves.

It's just a body and I wonder about
the transgression
for the King of the Woods
to have beheaded him.

Over the knoll is a mound of moss
brilliantly green as an Emerald City.
In a wheelbarrow lays a pile of slate
waiting to be a kingdom.

In the forest, I see shapes
of another dominion:
A bird with a crown of jewels.
A gazelle in a cape of gold.

A tree with long arms
reaches out. One hand
in the shape of *okay*
and the other one salutes me.

May

Spreading 30 bags of mulch, planting 25 hostas,
leveling bricks, rolling logs, raking leaves.
The black lab catches a baby bunny.
I shake my finger.
What a thing to do on Mother's Day.
He bows his head and follows
as I wrap the tiny body
in a napkin and place it in the earth.
Plan to paint the white septic pipes brown
to blend in with the trees.
A wild vine crawls the spine of a giant pine
and *sky* somehow now rhymes with *blue*.
In clandestine shadows, green ferns grow.
I only wish that they were red. In that old sad tale,
Billy found one between the canine graves
and took it as an omen.

My father lent me a book
narrated by a kidnapped collie
whose story broke our hearts in half.
A melancholic breeze washes through the air
with the scent of Le Muguet, Lily of the Valley,
my mother's favorite perfume.
Its pendant bells do not ring
but are silent as the bright and morning star.

Heart Math

3 hearts—1 heart does not=2
but rather a grove of trees
holding up the sky
the stars begging for forgiveness.

6 hearts÷3 also does not=2
but the chartreuse green
of a bush with bud.

The heart is never<nothing
is always>everything.

Heart^2 is a bird of paradise or
love x itself=light.

When stiff with grief
it forms a perfect triangle
every wall
a flawless match.

When velvet with bliss
its bell curve
rings true in the highest tower.

If you measure its chambers
you'll get the moon's circumference.

EVERY PAINTING HAS A DOOR

Road Trip

Oh, I might take a road trip through a town that caught on fire and find all the pieces that I've lost buried under ash. I could drive along the ocean's edge to a village in the hills and name it *there are brighter days ahead*. In this town is a giant bird larger than a tree, with wings named *how could you* and *I'm sorry that I did*. I'll drive some more and visit a museum where every painting has a door and a window that I'll open once I get inside. I might become a queen or a leopard that can fly or simply a woman knitting a road that goes nowhere.

Yellow

The moon above the road out winter's window,
lemons on the tray ready for tea, is the color
she saw days before Electric Shock Therapy.
I overheard my sister on the phone say to my mother
all I can see is yellow.
The look on my father's face
when he heard the same thing
was not yellow, but blood red.
The sun blazing across winter's field
that carries the fox, that carries the lab
running rampant through the snow.
Van Gogh's strange flowers and the wild
orbit of his mind. Her husband
beat her black and blue,
and as the bruises healed,
they turned yellow too.

Museum Study

In those days,
art was not yet a
window, had given up on
being a door. More suited to be
a staircase. Preferably bifurcated with
two options to ascend. Or maybe a cantilever
when steps to the height are open and dangerous with
nothing to prevent a fall. Never spiral, no need to save space
in art. Not straight but always circular to keep you dizzy. If you
are rich, art is a double staircase with live artists singing at the top.

Blood Work

The Two Fridas
Oil on canvas, 1939, Frida Kahlo

This is me and this is me.
One of us is dying.
The other is not.
We are tied by blood
and broken for each other.
In my blue dress, I clasp him.
You know who he is.
In my white dress,
I almost let my heart bleed out.
One vein, two hands connect me.
Have you ever held hands with death
while one of you is dying
and the other is not?

A Man We Used to Know

for R

He had a definitive
ease about him
that made you feel at rest,
a no-fuss, no-mess,
certain kind of man,
a chiseled handsome face,
and a swag of circumstance.

He'd drive the boat
and we'd sail away into
whitecaps of water and air.
If your floppy hat flew off,
he'd circle back around.
He was just that kind of man.

He always slightly
changed your name.
If you were Lisa,
he called you Lis.
If you were Suzie,
he called you Suze.
If you were Ann,
he called you Annie.
If you were Dustin,
he called you Dust.
If you were Brother,
he called you Bro.

If you were a walleye,
he would find you
or a buck lurking on the knoll.

Used to know is incorrect.
We know you and have known you
and will know you forever more.

Un

When she learned of his unfaithfulness,
she could not unsee their touching
but found some solace in a new uneven world.

Plucked deadheads off geraniums
said *at least I have this to do*
then went inside to stare out the window
at the unreliable view.

When evening came red flowers
drifted away into dark
she unplugged the past,
unmoored her heart
unmade her bed, unslept the night.

When daylight broke, she made up dreams
she wished that she had had,
observed her face, said *I am not unlovely*
though every doubt could never be undone.

When days, weeks, and months
passed by, she unfurled like
a fern in spring
then turned into the sun.

Narrative

The past and present got married one day
and had a baby named forever. She wore
a pink bonnet and had dimpled cheeks.

I wasn't invited to the wedding and neither were you
but we heard that the maid of honor carried
flowers only found in the fields of the future.

~ ~ ~

What was it that you were telling me when
your husband had an affair? It was something but
I don't recall. I just remember the look in your eyes.

The words came from your mouth and formed
inside a little balloon above your head. But you
were not cartoon-like and nothing was very funny.

~ ~ ~

Do you ever wonder about me now that you are dead?
How the story goes on like a baby in a bonnet, forever, how you,
just like yesterday and today, as much as you tried,
couldn't quite make it work?

Another Take at Happiness

i

a man on a green & yellow tractor
wearing a green & yellow ball cap,
an army green t-shirt, grey shorts, grey shoes,
a dog whistle around his neck. This time
the tractor has a backhoe. I cannot keep up
with all the attachments. He is leveling the
land where a mud bike track once was with
plans to plant wildflowers.

ii

a black lab wearing a bright orange collar,
chasing around the tractor,
tossing in the leaves,
rolling in the dirt,
smelling every leaf,
peeing on every tree.

iii

the same women in the same window
wearing the same shawl who should
be working and still
a field away from happiness

Happiness

I

a man in a plaid woolen shirt
a cigar in his mouth
a chainsaw in his hand
a black lab at his heels.

II

a black lab in a black fur coat
with a branch in his mouth
following a man
in a plaid woolen shirt.

III

a woman looking on from the window
with a shawl over her shoulders
a poem in her mouth
a field away from happiness
taking fodder from the view.

Notes for Survival

Like a rib remove A from *amen,* so Eve can eat the apple.
Drop B from *boat,* may you wildly sow your past.
Kiss and say goodbye when you release L from *lover.*
Unwed B from *bring,* then find a faithful partner.
Stay in the moment, melt S from *snow.*
Cast D from *dark* and be a boat of paws and whiskers
floating on the sea.
Minus O from *good* that you might learn to praise.
Loose N from *month* then fly, fly away.
Whirl into space like a sphere when G is
unearthed from *ground.*
Unfasten T from *heart* so you might learn to listen.
Let J escape from *jail* to find another way to grieve.
To be first in place, undo D from *wind.*
You will endure when something is taken
and take on a second life.

Memory

Fold yourself up; put yourself away
on the shelf amid the linens
in the drawer by the spatula—
the forgotten spoons and knives.

Make yourself a tool;
pry me open.
May the wicked
worst of you fly out.

Memory,
buy the house next door
so, I can borrow cups of you
when I am running out.

Turn yourself into a tree—
one that I can climb
to pick your lowest
hanging fruit.

Memory,
learn a foreign language then speak
to me in tongues. Set yourself on fire.
I'll put your ashes in an urn.

Tell me four stories.
One I want to remember
three I need to forget.

Song of July

A day goes by, and planes fly low to smoke out the furry moth.
    King Kong plays on TV, Jessica Lange in his palm.

A day goes by, a bunny appears every time I feel alone. The
    mountain ash have grown their berries, still green, waiting
    for the orange.

A day goes by, and a young clematis, mistaken for a weed, is
    thrashed down by the blade. A purple funeral procession
    leaves frail petals in the grass.

A day goes by, clouds spin round like a carousel in the sky. One, a
    white stallion, another, a big brown bear dressed up like a
    clown.

A day goes by, and a bullet sears the ear of a man
    who many abhor.

A day goes by and I am no less weary than I was
    the day before.

I Am Tired of Perfection

It is June, and I am tired of perfection
would rather just love the flaw of it all.
Dragonflies smother the stone angel's face;
the vine has strangled the rose.

Say what you will about order.
Heaven has no scheme.
God does not label and file our sins
but shreds their paper bodies,
then throws them to the wind.

Say what you will about Heaven.
The dead fly around in disheveled gowns.
The rich are still rich, and the poor are still poor.
Jesus' beard has grown far too long.

It is June, and I am tired of perfection.
Whatever tangles my heart,
tangle it more.
Dear Creeping Charlie, please
take over the lawn.

Notes

"Shadows" is after Alberto Rios

"Yellow" is after Charles Wright

"I Pledge Allegiance" is after Jackie Morris

"Falling" is after Jim Moore

"I am Tired of Perfection" is after Ann Sexton

"Notes for Survival" is after Rita Mae Reese

"Song of July" is after Nasser Rabah

"When Sorrow Sits with Me" is after Robert Frost

"Ars Poetica" is after Kenyatta Rogers

"The Poem is Open for Business" is after a quote by Deborah Keenan

About the Author

Ann Iverson is a writer and artist. She is the author of several poetry collections, a book of essays, and a series of children's books. Her poems have appeared on *Writer's Almanac,* and her poem "Plentitude" was set to a choral arrangement. Her artwork has been featured in a variety of venues. Ann continues to experiment with both visual and written art.

www.ingramcontent.com/pod-product-compliance
Lightning Source LLC
Chambersburg PA
CBHW072049160426
43197CB00014B/2689